The Wreck of Your Life on the Evening News

The Wreck of
Your Life
on the
Evening News

Poems

Roy Bentley

Sheila-Na-Gig Editions

Cover art: Gloria Regalbuto Bentley

ISBN: 9781962405195
Library of Congress Control Number: 2025937253

Sheila-Na-Gig Editions
Russell, KY
Hayley Mitchell Haugen, Editor
www.sheilanagigblog.com

Advance Praise

From the first, titular poem in this collection, Roy Bentley's readers know they're in a for a wild ride. Darkly funny, haunting, hopeful in spite of themselves, the poems in *The Wreck of Your Life on the Evening News* move deftly from the long-ago memory of a Doublemint kiss to questioning whether God is a grift, guiding us swiftly through youthful indiscretion—"sin and atonement, in that order"—until the dead begin to whisper and we slow down to listen, intently. Riffing through a crosscurrent undertone of American music, readers are led to a double rainbow rising over an historic battlefield, apt-enough metaphor for the spell these poems cast over a world "always up to its ass in war." A heart-shaped world, Bentley tells us, where "the Beautiful won't be contained and the Dead are in every / action we witness."

—Paula J. Lambert, author of *As If This Did Not Happen Every Day*

Those familiar with Roy Bentley's poetry immediately recognize his voice as being simultaneously intimate and worldly and distinctly Appalachian. In *The Wreck of Your Life on the Evening News*, Bentley's conversational, pull-no-punches style of storytelling weaves the histories of the United States, the Church, and even the geologic history of Earth with his own. The resulting tapestry of images and revelations explores what it means to be American in a time when defining that national identity is challenging at best and often at odds with the perspectives of friends and family and those nosy next-door neighbors who are ever eager to question "the promise of freedom" we are all sold.

—Chuck Salmons, author of *The Grace of Gazing Inward*

Acknowledgments

I want to thank the editors of the literary magazines where these poems first appeared:

BarBar: "Starman"

Broad River Review: "(Sometimes I Feel) Like a Red-collared Dog"

Delmarva Review: "Kissing"

The Dillydoun Review: "The Faithful Account of How, in the Chill of October-Ohio, a Sweet Corn Queen Thanks Our Lord and Savior Jesus Christ"

The Lakeshore Review: "Double Rainbow above the Little Bighorn Battlefield"

Laurel Review: "Autumn Leaves"

Lost Pilots: "Poem in Praise of Surviving My Life"

Michigan Quarterly Review: "My Sister Stephanie Returns as a Mad, High Laugh"

Northern Appalachia Review: "All the Pretty Little Horses as Eschatology" and "On Finding Out My Bastard-Father's Half-brothers and Half-sisters Were Protective of Him as a Child in Kentucky"

Passengers Journal: "The Wreck of Your Life on the Evening News"

Pine Mountain Sand & Gravel: "Hey, That's No Way to Say Goodbye"

Santa Fe Writers Project: "Monsters"

Silver Rose Magazine: "Leaf-fall in October in Ohio"

takahē: "Honesty"

The Vincent Brothers Review: "Mating Turtles Fossilized in the Act," "Surrealistic Pillow," and "Pain"

Contents

To Cait, with love in hard times. . . .

The Wreck of Your Life on the Evening News

If the anchorman got excited about whatever bad thing
it was, repeating the list of dead and injured, you knew;
mostly, that what happened was almost entirely on you.

You'd need a lawyer who resembled Abraham Lincoln.
Someone from the eastern-Kentucky backwoods whose
great-great-great-grandfather was shot at least 20 times

his final night on earth for trying to arrest a moonshiner.
Anyway, you fucked up. Big time. And someone died.
Someone else wound up a ghost from the waist down.

The death car, oodles of gore on the seats, a Plymouth,
there on the *CBS Evening News with Walter Cronkite*.
You were famous. Which is to say, famously screwed.

Your nephew saw it—the fatal-car-crash screen footage
on the evening news. Complete with footage of the blood-
and-brain-spatter, the rest of the mayhem you had caused.

He ushered a son away from the TV. Offered a magazine.
Mercy was the *Playboy* opened to distract your kid with
breasts summoning like some kind of roadside signage.

Kissing

Under a light bulb in Pat Leahy's basement,
under the spell of the tepid enchantment she
may feel on rising from a place in the circle
of adolescents drinking and playing Truth

or Dare, Jody McLaughlin answers someone
daring her to kiss The Fat Kid in Dress Khakis.
And I extend my neck, juvenile hawk that I am,
to grapple with the expectations of a mouth

on my mouth. I'm fifteen, and this is Ohio.
It's not my first pubescent-kiss, but it's close.
Nineteen sixty-nine is the usual mysteries and
lawn jobs to do and Plane Geometry homework,

everyone in the basement as clueless as it gets.
But who would refuse Experience with Hendrix
playing "Hey Joe" as Jody loses her Doublemint?
I wind up sharing the taste of the gum, though

she's palmed it, the wad, apologetically, deftly,
just prior to lipsticked lips and sweetened tongue
asking to be remembered after death or long enough
to cancel all that isn't worth remembering in any case.

South Chanute Street (1974)

We're talking small: a two-bedroom trailer, where
the living room might have held about a dozen folks.
We're smoking Thai sticks. Doing pharmaceuticals.
It's obvious that one of the airmen is quite stoned.
To the point he's pissed himself. The spot spreads,
keeps spreading—in nineteen seventy-four Shaft
is the Man. Richard Roundtree. This guy looks
like Richard Roundtree. Nevertheless, there are

at least two Americas: one can handle its drugs.
What we did after that—I'll let you put yourself
in his place: you've smoked till you feel God lean
down to whisper, Enough, kiddo. But then you go
over to the stereo. Maybe put on Traffic and check
yourself. And then, if you're a Guy Who Looks Like
Richard Roundtree, you say, *Apparently I've pissed
myself.* In that banal voice you use to elicit mercy.

On the Grand Staircase of the RMS *Titanic*

If the existence of God is more than a grift,
my Divinity descends the Grand Staircase of

the RMS *Titanic* in a gown of light celebrating
brash, wild infinities of Time and timelessness.

The Grand Staircase of RMS *Titanic* is restored.
God travels it like she owns the White Star Line,

if not the entire eleven-dimensional Multiverse—
if there's a grift, it starts here. The outright lies

of evangelicals earn her best clandestine-laughter.
I'd have asked Magnificence to risk the fish-nets,

but it's First Class. Besides, she's always emerging
to gasps, anyway. A striking lady, I step to meet her.

She takes my arm. She reminds me of a wading bird:
loads of decorous wing-play come down to flight-blur.

Tonight, she could pronounce Doom's secret name but
likely won't share it, the name, with anyone breathing.

My Sister Stephanie Returns as a Mad, High Laugh

My sister Stephanie returns as the mad, high laugh
from someone who got her to vote for Barack Obama.

Now she's back as the squirrel gorging on gift-cashews
and gossiping (to itself) on the subject of Ohio winters.

And that's her as a schmaltzy Sinatra song—"Luck Be
a Lady"—on XM Channel 71: *Luck be a lady tonight.*

Then she's the finite space between saxophone notes,
a part of the soul resolving as the long-held last breath

finally expelled. Next, back she comes as the marijuana
she left behind: Golden-State-drought-dry but smokable.

Now she's the Kodak of a blond one-year-old dragging
a Fisher-Price phone across a black-tile floor, mugging

for Mother's birthday-gift Brownie box camera, posing
in a pair of hard-soled white shoes then as the reverse-

sunset on that framed photograph of her on the mantel
where light is particularly fractious but engoldening.

The Satisfaction Theory of Atonement

A street of tiered houses butted up against
a Tilt-a-Whirl red glow near Coffman's Farm.
Dirt-and-grass parking. A makeshift midway.

The rows of tents were lit by Christmas bulbs,
the white ones, which sagged above the games
of chance, a tribute to the vicissitudes of fortune.
Everything was pumpkin-candled from dusk on.

By a state route sign there was another sign.
A woman's caricature, a carnival stripper
or the reasonable facsimile. Of course

this carnival stripper didn't strip—she was
there because someone would make a buck,
and she only unpeeled to her bra and panties
to some songs from a tape deck: Gypsy Rose

Lee minus spinner-tassels and the big-hair wig.
I was 12, and I wanted to see. But I didn't want
to be Lost, a sinner. I thought of Virgil Horsley,

a preacher at First Baptist Heath, and his sermon
entitled The Satisfaction Theory of Atonement.
I didn't want it—theology—in my head. And so
I paid. Heard "Stand back, everyone stand back!"

then some tinny parody of the Burma Shave theme
and or Bobby Darin talk-singing "Mack the Knife"
while a conflagrational bonfire burned outside.

I remember toothy jack-o-lantern shadows
badged the woman bumping and grinding
at a bunch of us learning lust and guilt,
if not sin and atonement, in that order.

Castro, Crossing a Street in New York in Fatigues, Hands Out Cuban Cigars

I'm aware that my garage-door installer,
Angel Rodriguez (born in Cuba) liked it,
his life after the Cuban Revolution. I recall
Angel moralizing about Cuba's health care.
This was before ACA, and before Obama—
so he was rubbing salt into wounds he
understood Americans had to endure.

I admitted that I could see his poin—
if his point was Fidel is treasured.
I said Fidel had gone too far.
I said the phrase *too far* without
drama or shaking my head. Nothing.
But I was thinking, in particular, of Che
Guevara having to leave Cuba for Bolivia

where the CIA had its operatives murder him
then send the hands to Cuba as proof of death.
The fact that he was new to South Florida,
Angel Rodriguez Garage Door Installer,
was no excuse for committing the sin
of causing me to praise Fidel Castro.
And on a Tuesday, which Gabriel

Garcia Marquez tells us is when
the world turned sad—the day an
angel the villagers will treat badly
suddenly shows up out of nowhere.
Which, now that I reconsider it, is God
Mother God in the Sky That Motherfucker
telling us that's where all of us show up from.

Why if You Put a Hat and Glasses on a Dog, He Looks Like He Could Drive a Truck

—Dave Attell

First, the Wayfarer sunglasses are pretty awesome.
Ready an iPhone, though the Wayfarers *are* the gag.

Each dog is a set of uncertainties in need of an owner
with a flat-bed truck full of patience. I have to wonder

why any creature tolerates a human. Isolation gets old,
sure, and an Astros baseball cap never looked better

backwards on a Golden Retriever with skin issues.
In 1926, Clemington Corson was the first mommy

and second woman to swim the English Channel—
now, try not to imagine her putting her goggles

on a pooch awaiting her return like she's Jesus
or Jesus' channel-swimmer sister whose love

is an immense deal. Pat pat. Pat fucking pat.
After the mutt-touching, out comes the hat.

Rocket Man

So, I had this dream where a friend of mine
parks a rocket ship in my backyard and asks me
not to touch it or go inside or ask why it's there.
I have a good-sized backyard, but his ship is big
and takes up some space. I tell him, I guess. Sure.
And ask him how long he'll need to park it there.
He says, I had to land in a hurry. I'm not sure.
He's a good friend, so I wave it off and we
go inside my house. I keep looking back,
at this silver thingamabob catching the
afternoon sunlight—it's like the ship
in the movie *Forbidden Planet*: shiny
and finned and standing as upright as
the promise of freedom from want that
all exploration has had from its inception.
I've got nosy neighbors. Sure enough, one
rings the doorbell and asks, excitedly, whether
he can have a look at the craft. My friend answers
before I can say anything about security clearances.
And this goes on—the doorbell ringing, the two of us
answering questions, my good friend shaking his head
and smiling like he swallowed a happy pill or it's payday
and we're going drinking at the bar that has great Reubens.
It's a dream, and so I don't ask questions beyond how long
I have to accede to having a two-story uber-marvel parked
and looking all-radiant in the usually diffuse Ohio sunlight.
He doesn't know, anyway. Says that's what friends are for.
We head off to the bar with the Reubens, though he doesn't
eat meat or offer explanation as to why my backyard. This
is one of those dreams where you let a thing be what it is.
This is a reminder some relationships are what they are,
and you can yard-park a rocket ship without hesitation.

(Sometimes I Feel) Like a Red-collared Dog

So I go to Herbology on 21st Street
in Newark, Ohio—I left my wife Gloria
in the Prius and went inside and got hit on,
hair something off of Gandalf's Facebook page
and 68 years old—don't condescend to this wizard.
He still has most of his teeth and everything functions.
I built him from a kit. That Guy went home. Ate dinner
and turned down an invite-call from the check-in woman.
I know this is one more poem and Chris Rock is tweeting
about his slap in the kisser at the Oscars, but it happened.

A new law wants dangerous-breed dogs in New York
to wear special red collars. The animals are to be taxed
and registered. Their numbers controlled. Understandably.
For a long time now, I've felt that, with regard to monogamy.
Like a red-collared dog: like I have almost no business around
certain other humans—in my case, Women—without at least
reminded that, in my case, the lass in the Prius saved my life.
And she loves me. And goddamn it, anyway: some dogs
never learn. Some dogs need red-collared and watched.
This one will wear the collar of this poem and howl.

Atheist Turned Evangelist Turned College Teacher Lectures on Original Sin and the Comma Splice

She has a bone to pick with the State of Texas and
with the Catholic Church and a complicit America
for telling her what to do with Her Body before and
during and or after sex, consensual or not. However,
she was raised to believe in the inherent goodness of
humanity and an ordered-though-mysterious Universe
in which America isn't only the spawn of butcher-Brits
who made laws to control trade in indigenous peoples.

A blackboard-sample pleads misogyny before the bar
of secular ethics: *First Woman had no idea First Man
was as clueless as he turned out to be, he would blame
her for getting them kicked out of Paradise for sharing
an apple.* She wants the State of Texas to kiss her ass.
Still, she knows the Game—and so her lady parts will
get in line. Nevertheless, this one quotes Elvis Costello,
a singer, saying there's no such thing as an original sin.

Hey, That's No Way to Say Goodbye

—Leonard Cohen

I was 25 when a friend said, Lose the sunglasses at night.
Gradient tinted wire-rims like ones John Lennon sported.

I may have told him to fuck himself, but I heard him out.
In this life, you don't want to be an ass. Or listen to one.

A bully of a kind men know. Women, too. Reminded me,
then, of that mistral-Suzanne in the song: he made tea and

shared a variety of orange come all the way from China,
but he acted like his presence was a gift or, for you, lucky.

In his defense, we were the same age; though I was married,
and so I couldn't roam nightlife-streets in our college town.

This was nineteen seventy-nine. Jimmy Carter was president.
Me and this guy were friends. And friends will presume shit

about you. Maybe he was busting balls, as they used to say;
and maybe I never cared that much for the company of men.

I can't blame him for thinking that he could hand me advice:
he was from Cleveland, which knows it's tougher than the rest

of the brokenhearted rust-belt cities of the American Midwest.
Oh: and he said he flushed my self-published book of poetry

down his American Standard toilet. Said it like he'd done me
a great kindness—which, now that I think of it, maybe he had.

Mating Turtles Fossilized in the Act

> The oldest known vertebrates to be fossilized
> while mating are a pair of 47 million-year-old turtles
> attached by their genitals as they got buried alive.
>
> —CNN

In the case of the turtles on the *National Enquirer*,
it must've been one truly conflagrational moment.

Meaning mid-coitus the earth opens. Swallows you.
Ahead in the Kroger line, a youngish mother with

inquiring-minded small children soft-smacks hands.
And then I say, Maybe they're thinking ET: the eyes.

Nothing better than feeling yourself trying to be kind
unless you count imagining that love transcends Time.

My first love and I ran into each other some years ago.
By then, both of us were married. Happy or mostly so.

It wasn't in Kroger, but it could've been. She said, we
should go someplace. Meaning, And fuck. She crooned

my name, which was pleasant to hear. As honey-sweet
as hearing there's sex after death and you'll be having

some—like the turtles whose love will last for as long
as rivers run and a form of kindness curbs our tongues.

Worst Street Magician in Neon, Kentucky, Demonstrates the Difference between Dirt Poor & Dirt Poor with Pride

A friend I made one summer in Kentucky said he dreamed
of being a magician. I helped him set up an outhouse door
on sawhorses for a stage. He talked Houdini, performed.

Buster Collins couldn't pull a rabbit out of a hat because
no one who lived in a row house could afford a top hat.
He said they kill songbirds, magicians, surrendering

tiny bodies to the Trick when collapsing the cages.
He draped a cage (minus the bird) then flattened it—
this is the part of the poem where I say something

about capitalism to melt your hard, American heart:
Buster had Magic Markered *Buster the Great* onto
the shirt his father would likely whip him for using.

He wore it draped, the shirt. Tied around his neck.
And palmed a quarter pulled from my Yankee ear.
I heard he went to work in the mines, Buster—his

father had black lung; he couldn't work. Not saying
that you can't sacrifice a few sparrows in hopes that
shared prosperity starts breaking out like a pandemic.

But calling what some are handed Choice is a trick,
a sleight of hand making the practitioner a magician
who couldn't care less about the fate of songbirds.

All the Pretty Little Horses as Eschatology

Claire McCoy told me the actor William Holden
stepped onto the edge of his bathtub, stone drunk,

with wet feet, and broke his neck in a resulting fall.
She laughed. Claire loved to laugh. She asked if I

had a condom. I said, Yes. She might've smiled.
That was the same night she sang "All the Pretty

Little Horses"—I read her a James Wright poem
says we break into blossom at the instant of death.

Though it's a form of wishful thinking, that poem,
any poem, really, she asked to have it read to her,

"A Blessing," a few years later, as she was dying.
This is me reminding you, Claire McCoy: at least

you didn't die like William Holden, goose stepping
through the eschatology of the Endless: red asterisk

on some list to remind us providence is far from fair.
This is me hearing you call out to God on the stairs.

In the Money Luck Wanted Hotel

If there's such a thing as the Celestial
Drapery, my dead mother pulled it back.
You bet: That Drape. She said my name.
This occurred the other day by the fridge:

an extortionate, top-of-the-line Whirlpool—
what I previously thought about the afterlife
is for another poem. I felt a low-voiced Roy
and remembered in the film *Princess Bride*

Billy Crystal giving us Dead or Mostly Dead.
I stood in a kitchen in the May light, shaking.
Same woman once offered: God has a place
and He / She should know it and stay in it—

honestly, the voice wasn't pissed off enough
to be the mother I knew. My hillbilly mother.
Who reddened my father's face with a sandal,
beat me with a leather belt for laughing at her.

If the bio metaphysics of anger does outlast us,
it may carry us like any moment of good fortune
or luck. How much truth do you want, these days?
Should I remind you how love breaks all the rules?

Be that as it may, I heard what I heard: my uber-
enraged mom beatific or mostly and, somehow,
extant enough to weak-whisper in my bad ear.
I have to tell you, I wouldn't put it past her.

Vroom

I don't remember if I wrote about my
cousin Bob Ramsdail's last phone message,
or when or where I retrieved it, either a poem
with the word *elegy* in the title, something nice,
or a short story with a character modeled after him,
Bob, who shaved a cat once as an adult man and liked
Rush Limbaugh, explaining that Rush made sense to him.

Not saying he was an ass, this cousin I loved like a brother.
I'm saying he thought for himself, risking scorn from family
and friends. I gave him a pretty hard time about Rush, sure.
Bob claimed to know Plainly Stupid when he heard it or
witnessed it enacted anywhere in or around Lima, Ohio.
He made a vroom sound. Said, "It's a guy who makes
that sound-marker for a muscle car but doesn't drive."

I stuck a finger into my open mouth. Gagged. Said:
Stupid is as Stupid does, my momma always said—
which made him laugh. He's dead now, my cousin
Bob whose last message reminded me he believed
in Jesus Christ as his personal savior and told me
he loved me. That he'd see me again soon. Which
is unlikely, sure, but—*vroom!*—I hope is true.

Pain

God is a concept by which we measure our pain.

—John Lennon

It's 1965. Up and down Dorothy Lane,
there are gargantuan signs for McDonald's
and J.C. Penney's—Beatles music is playing
in the passing cars. A stop-sign-red Ford pulls
into a parking space and a mother and boy-child
exit. How do I know? Because I'm the boy-child.
I'm starting off months of dental work. In a blue,
foot-activated dentist's chair that first day, I give

the universal sign for Pain, waving off the drilling.
The dentist registers an *uh-huh* and goes back to it,
time elongating like a black hole has just opened
near Huffman Prairie where the Wright Brothers,
Wilbur and Orville, learned to fly. The Bookmobile
shelves a biography detailing aeronautical struggles.
I remember reading something like: *Orville Wright
killed a co-pilot some years after Wilbur died of flu,*

the trauma staying with Orville the rest of his life.
My suffering ends for the day. I leave the office
and its medicinal stench. And look up like I'm
searching the sky. Catholics believe that pain
is our ticket on a train to Paradise no amount
of blood sacrifice ever touches, Redemption
a thing to be addressed sooner rather than later.
Like the rough reconstruction of a bad tooth.

I don't want to grow accustomed to pain, but
I'm Appalachian, and so that's just what I do,
my Appalachian mother telling me Walk it off
as we get in the red Ford she bought herself
after a hard-fought separation and divorce.
There. At least she turns on the radio and—
thank you, Jesus!—sings along as she drives,
the ubiquity of sunlight her new middle name.

Surrealistic Pillow

Second album out of the gate. Such babies
but big with West Coast university-crowds.
And I remember my friend Butch Thompson
holding the jacket, laughing at "White Rabbit"—
my Black trailer-mate in nineteen seventy-three;
this ten years after Muhammad Ali reminded us,
in Louisville, and in a Kentucky department store
catering to whites, that being Black is a good thing.
I didn't know it then, but young-Ali was bankrolled
by a group of wealthy white men to protect him from
such shit. And to make those rich white men money.
Butch respected Ali for saying *Go fuck yourself*—
to the Draft, though we were in the Air Force then.
I'd have to say Butch acted like we were learning,
white people, in those days. Which I believed too.
We were friends, and he liked that I'd get high and
clean. Dust, sweep. Disappear a day's dirty dishes.
But my mother ordered me not to bring him home
to Ohio. Which schooled us both. He was saying
I could know him. Be his friend then. However,
being a Black-American in nineteen seventy-three
would be the one record he wouldn't turn me on to.
That bit of housekeeping I'd accomplish on my own.

Why the Last Snow on Earth May Be Red
(for Al Maginnes)

> The color comes from astaxanthin, a molecular cousin of
> the chemical that makes carrots orange. The algae produce
> it seemingly as a sunscreen; it absorbs UV light, warming
> the organisms, and, critically, melting the surrounding
> snow.
>
> —Alan Burdick, *The New Yorker*

XM was playing Bruce Springsteen's "The Promised
Land" from the '78 Tour, where I caught his act once.

(Sure. We rocked that colosseum—or, rather, Bruce and
the E Street Band did, and we followed his lead.) Anyway,

I had a university reading scheduled the next day and was
catching up with my past or letting it catch up with me.

Look. If you want to know something about this life—
like: why in the hell the last snow on earth may be red—

don't look to me for answers. Maybe the last snow will
be like a song: it'll take you somewhere. *I ain't a boy,*

no I'm a man / And I believe in a promised land…
Maybe life is a train and then suddenly—snap your

fingers—the train is gone. Let me say it another way:
I was listening to Bruce Springsteen at the end of a day

I'd wanted to die, and he reminded me not to despair.
Maybe stick around. See the world turn a blood-red.

Sweet Lorraine

The woman must be just shy of drop-dead gorgeous,
given any of the interpretations of the great jazz standard,
especially Tony Bennett's version with ukulele and clarinet
or Nat King Cole's nonstop miracle with Oscar Peterson on
the piano and Coleman Hawkins on sax, the coffin of Beauty
opened like being this particular iteration of Woman, hers,
is a daily forever-resurrection. Not to mention the sex.
You can hear Actuality brought to a kind of fruition.

If you lean against Memory's glass-topped case,
even at 67, with you glimpsing death in every song
and heartbeat-and-breath—Death with her small breasts
the song of resolute movement and Love, wave-shaped lips
parting to pronounce one whole lifetime of stupidity as the
prelude to a blessing, the air resonant with Womanhood—
you can almost feel her earnest hand on yours, the grave
explained as a promise of abiding charity continuing.

The Faithful Account of How, in the Chill of October-Ohio, a Sweet Corn Queen Thanks Our Lord and Savior Jesus Christ

Maybe she is Midwest-beautiful, but if the
Mormons had their way, she'd be Head Wife
and advocate praying for the souls of the dead.

The Catholics are a whole other order of angel.
And the Baptists who speak of Hell, forgetting
Perdition has more than one zip code, including

this one. She's riding in a Caddy with local-hero
driver, hand-lettered posterboard placard-signage
giving the whys and wherefores for the hullabaloo.

When the Cadillac stops, she accepts a microphone.
It doesn't hurt she has abundant breasts more than
temperamentally suited to Celebrity Star Status—

Crest 3D Whitening Strips bleached teeth flash,
a reminder that here, in Ohio, Beauty is a woman
tugging down her mini-skirt-length dress, waving.

She's handed a bouquet of roses. Steps up to thank
Our Lord and Savior Jesus Christ, drawing applause
and handing off the mic. She climbs back in the car

to a refrain of small dogs on studded leashes barking
as if to warn of dangers nearer at hand than any hell.

Monsters

Most who became monsters turned back into people
after a few weeks, but some, sadly, did not.
  —Teddy Wayne, "The Age of Monsters" (*The New Yorker*)

I caught Lon Chaney's wolfman act. I saw Bela Lugosi, too.
A lot of *Dracula* and *Frankenstein* and *Son of Frankenstein*—

whatever the doctor was trying to restore began with a spark
then came alive at about the giga-voltage of a lightning strike.

But there's also the monster my father could become after booze
before he left us. In the movie of our life, he never made it back

to human form. There are fathers and then there are men leaving
you with a desolate adult—like a kid knows how to help a mother

keep it together and get off her ass. Be daring again, having been
abandoned with kids. He's dead, my impenitent father, so what

good is saying shit-anything about any of it? Nothing, I guess.
Unless, by some fairylike magic, you add him showing me

love begins with being around. And not just at Christmastime,
when love is a fistfight (or the threat of one) at 2808

Comanche, a couple of Cadillacs in the asphalt drive
and a '48 Mercury coupe he promises he'll restore—

under the billowing tarp beneath the carport roof
by headstones dated after the Revolutionary War,

headstones he rolled down a hill for trash cans
to rest upon, saying, No one was using them.

Ella Fitzgerald Sings "The Dipsy Doodle"

YouTube says it was a "#1 hit for Tommy Dorsey in 1937"—
and Bill Haley and His Comets have a version. Sometimes

a singer owns a song. Janis Joplin's "Me & Bobby McGee"
or Billie Holiday dressing the trees of the American South

in strange fruit. This is Ella's song: Ella is saying to forget
certitude. Not that cluelessness is a virtue. No fucking way.

As any Black woman in America, the vocalist knows more
than she is at liberty to say. Because saying all, or any part,

of what she knows about this hard country can get her killed.
If the Powers That Be detest what you say, talk in metaphors.

Certitude will fall from you like the coat from your shoulders,
and you'll sing of a man in love with a woman who is in love

with some other man. The definition of the Dipsy Doodle.
Like Ella, your song will be preaching that we are changed

once by what we struggle not to let touch us. And, once more,
that portion of our unhappy history finds us out, regardless.

Leaf-fall in October in Ohio

"Shut up and die like an aviator."
—Steve Earle

Time and wind do most of the work, leaves
being bio-inclined to live and then die. Your
job (and mine) to pay attention once more.
To bystander mid-fall. And the landings.

If there is a soundtrack to Falling, and
there is, it includes motorcycle engines.
And rock 'n roll and rap songs dispersed
from passing convertibles, the tops down,

the temperature of the ambient outside-air
pretty fucking great, to borrow an Ohioism.
If nothing else, the mechanisms of leaf-fall
reveal passing with a bit of grace: to shut up

about Sorrow and Grief and just die. Oh, and
like an aviator—if you're Orville Wright who
sat stunned at Ohio leaf-fall after seeing oceans
of spinning, light-struck trajectories from above.

Under Fire, Out of Fuel, No Air Support

We're never as completely full of shit as when we're at war.
Bullets don't solicit a motive as they rip into heart- or lung-

or child-flesh; they make no allowance for correctness of
cause or the nationalities of soldiers on the receiving end.

It may be pleasant to think something principled under fire
and out of fuel and without air support. On the other hand,

at the heart of war is nationalism. And nationalism is, first
last and always, reducible to wanting not to die in pain and

crying out, alone. It's wanting to feel a part of something.
Something good. But this world has had a gun to its head

for so long that some will shout *Kill me!* Enough threats.
Enough talk of our terrible histories. Enough imagining.

To quote an old Elmore James song: *The sky is crying*.
To elegize from the song: *I've got a bad, bad feeling*.

Near My 60th Birthday, I Answer a Report That I Used to Be Quite the Ladies Man

I'm teaching at a technical college in a coal town
in Ohio when one of my students approaches me.
He's smiling like he has fake-swallowed Ye Olde
Canary. An immense grin. Which pisses me off.
Something about my sexual behavior in my 40s.
It's none of his business what the hell I did then,
but an educator is a sort of public person, and so

I laugh out loud and tell him I'll give the author
of that stirring rumor twenty American dollars
to keep repeating it. Which makes him laugh,
proving that it's better to be thought Funny
than a sexual conquistador, any day. Which
ends it. Unless you add in my having to run
the movie of my life backwards for days after—

one nominee said she longed for respect: for the
moment of her death to be a big deal to someone.
I had to work the next day and so needed sleep
but I listened and I was wide awake when she
fell asleep and snored and I dressed to leave
but then looked back at her, hypothesizing
how I might lie to myself and just be him,

the guy living for her next and next breath.
And I undressed and slipped back into bed.
Which was wrong. For both of us, I guess.
Unless you count all the times I'd watched
and she woke up and caught me watching
and felt what you feel that isn't quite love
but answers some portion of our longing.

Autumn Leaves

I miss fall in New England, says the shipwrecked couple in
one of the cartoons in *The New Yorker* I'm reading in reverse.
"Autumn Leaves" is on the commercial-free-radio jazz station.
What do you need to hear about Miles that you haven't heard?
That he and Sonny Stitt couldn't stand each other but played
together in London and Paris and Rome, Sonny's saxophone

and Miles' iconic trumpet worth a little quarrel. Or that Miles
performed the song a lot in 1960 when he first wrote his version.
That the music teacher I knew once, from Iowa, who taught for
Ohio State, said her boyfriend Mark named a son after Miles.
As if every other white-guy-who-loves-bebop-jazz fan hadn't
beaten him to the punch. Across the world, there's a war on.

In their basement-shelters Ukrainians are huddled, listening
to whatever lifts the mood of beaten-down and too-soon-slain.
All God's creatures may well be destroyed by fire and by ice;
given that this new warfare is the old warfare amended, War
an acquired skill much like the practice of tolerance and love
on the other end of the spectrum. You blow shit up to learn

how to blow shit up. Leaving unanswered the question
of the chances of nuclear war breaking out, I'm reminded
that the question is unanswerable in the best of times.
And I turn up Miles Davis and Sonny Stitt, picturing
the inimitable gold of oak leaves cascading down
and—oh God of Mercy, God of Doom—down.

Joy Tears Is What They Call Them

Merle Haggard sings that his—joy tears
is what they call them—have everything to do
with his mommy and daddy. Memories of them.
Merle says the spigots of feeling will crank open—
that it's one big Get out your handkerchiefs, mister.
Meaning he cries. A man, I'm guessing, who's heard
Credence Clearwater Revival and so would understand
tearing up at *a dinosaur Victrola listening to Buck Owens.*

I used to get them watching certain John Wayne westerns.
Because I'd glimpsed his idea of America. And bought it.
A few months before he left us, John Wayne was handed
a .38. Weak and in agony. Lung cancer, the second time.
He handed it back, the pistol. (Had someone do it, more
likely.) Saying: *John Wayne doesn't shoot John Wayne.*
As if his birth-name wasn't Marion Robert Morrison
and he was another guy now, the one in the movies.

Loud Hillbilly at a Bob Dylan Concert

I've been this guy—who am I kidding?
I've taken Vicodin & then drank a beer.
If buzzed is a precondition to Enlightenment,

I'm a goofy fuck in jeans & a t-shirt in spring.
Now I call out for the song "Chimes of Freedom"
like Dylan may've forgotten he wrote that one.

All right, I did leave the moonshine in the Prius,
but the Prius is bumper-stickered BIDEN HARRIS
& BLACK LIVES MATTER. I might as well be

Guy of a Certain Age shouting at a stage between
numbers. However, then he nods & kicks off
a quasi-version of "Chimes of Freedom" like

I've been heard by Bob, even if my parents
are hillbillies whose lives are best described as
spellbound & swallowed until the tolling ended...

Sandy

We're neighbors on the same cul-du-sac in small-town Ohio.
She waves. Smiles. Tosses a Frisbee my way. I catch it and,

that summer, somewhere between one thing and the next,
Sandy is walking with me. There are fresh pleasure-shivers

as she pronounces my name. And I'm thinking that first love
should be like any bundle of perfumed letters acknowledged,

happily, at mail call in Air Force Basic Training at Lackland.
Sweet-smelling letters arrived like clockwork at first. Then

she fell for a guy with a motorcycle who she started to see
before I was gone a month. Maybe that's the way things go—

but envelopes passed from the drill sergeant's hand to mine,
one giddy airman pleading, *Hey, let me get a whiff!* before

being hooted at by the rest of the barracks, then waved off.
Like remembrances of certain lovers after enough time.

The Afterlife of Ed Potter

Big Mary's Place is famous for shootings. If there's a native
tongue spoken by those in the hills, then it's Constant Sorrow.
My mother will pray for my unsaved soul and the rotten world.
A great blue heron will fly down onto her postage-stamp yard.
Junior? He's going to choke on a toothpick—you heard me.
Sure, it makes sense Junior Tucker shot me—to say *Ed
Potter is mean* would be like saying It's raining. Meaning
something in the nature of Levi Frank Potter's boys keeps us

fighting and scratching when someone else might tell himself
that if, in some reasonable amount of time, you don't succeed,
forget it. Back off. Potter men don't do that: back off. Junior
knew that. He didn't want to bloody-up his store-bought shirt,
so out comes a .38 pistol. And it (flash-*bang!*) put a hole in me.
Ask anyone in Letcher County, Kentucky. Say, *Pack a lunch
you fight a Potter.* See if he doesn't grin like he gets the joke.
See if his smile isn't the sort to sire opponents and opposition.

On Finding Out My Bastard-Father's Half-brothers and Half-sisters Were Protective of Him as a Child in Kentucky

It doesn't explain his hatred for his father. The clenched jaw
he'd wear whenever he talked about Bob Beach. Or a tear—

whisperings may have been news of the father who limped
because it only takes once to say far too much to some men.

It didn't make much difference who brought it up; he just
declined to hear it mentioned, even without judgment or

condescension. He'd flip out if we broached the subject.
He's ten years dead and well-buried when I hear that his

half-brothers and -sisters looked out for him growing up.
That they put movie money in his small hand at the Neon

or motioned to the usher to let him through without paying—
pictures like *Wild West Days* with Johnny Mack Brown whose

tin-star sheriff had Kentucky in his name. A talent for gunplay.
I know now there is a private linguistics to sorrow and shame.

He wasn't the homeliest boy in Fleming-Neon grade school,
my father, and no one picked on him without answering for it,

so the archaeology of his life wasn't unearthed by me or anyone.
I don't speak Bastard or Hillbilly, but when he spoke I listened—

in neon-lit darknesses or on the streets of small Kentucky towns
wherein our American language fights not to fail us but then does.

Often, he said it wasn't any of our goddamn business. The protocol:
every spigot of memory opened was his to close without explanation.

She Walks Till the Water Is Too Deep to Stand in, Then Pulls Her Legs Up and Floats

—Allen Bratton, "Philippa," The Sewanee Review:
Volume CXXX, Number 1

Her older brother would like to think himself upstaged by
how she entered the country of her dying—it's like Steph
booked a rocket ship without saying she was going into
Space. Sometimes now I see my sister enter the state of
breathlessness and hushed quiet as if it were a spring lake:
She walks till the water is too deep to stand in, then pulls
her legs up and floats—can you see her? Swanlike, then a
chubby-kid, then young and Ohio-beautiful with an attitude.

A woman in the 1990s, she fell for a guy named Clayton
who beat her, although she didn't let on until he was gone.
Who knows, maybe I did say, *You two ought to get married*
and pick up the dinner check in that bar on Buckeye Lake.
I loaned him three hundred dollars once because of her,
so they wouldn't lose their house. He asked me nice and
I liked that he left the table and went out into winter-Ohio
darkness to warm up his red Ford F-150 for my sister.

Hard Night in Fleming-Neon

Any night our bunch sat up with one of their dead,
someone might break out a Mason jar of moonshine.

Kinfolk would bunk in the row houses in Fleming—
with other family who hadn't fled Letcher County.

Once, I cut high school after they left me behind
in our adopted home-country of Ohio. I borrowed

a fire-engine-red '64 Ford Galaxie 500 XL—Mark
Chapman and Mike and Tom Kozlowski and me.

News of our truancy arrived during Calling Hours
when Old Regular Baptists sang and praised Jesus.

And I heard it ruined Uncle Howard's big sendoff:
my uncle with a Pure Oil station at Neon Junction

who'd given my pops a job, at 7, pumping gasoline.
Mother's mean, older brother Bill volunteered. Said

he'd make the run to New Mexico to fetch us back.
He didn't come for us, though, and we spent days

on the backroads; stopping in Hannibal, Missouri
where I snatched a copy of *Life on the Mississippi.*

Seemed the thing to do: sunset by the Mississippi
aflame and burning like a swallow of moonshine.

76° Fahrenheit Rain Coming

It was Ohio in June: Don't like the weather? Wait.
Rain fell in a way thunderstorms have of letting slant-
downpours curtain frontier and the smooth face of water.
After, I walked through a mostly-clover backyard with
my grandson. It was the week of his first birthday, his
second visit. He'd plucked a clover flower. Eaten it.

I was vaccinated. The two-shot Moderna. Had worn
a mask, lathered up my hands until I felt like Enough.
Not sure about the balance of America. Ohio was tired.
We could've used a week at a beach in south Florida
where the skies open in afternoons in June and rain
rinses the air so clean you picture angels at work.

Double Rainbow above the Little Bighorn Battlefield

The air above the white marble marking the boneyard
brightened above where Sioux & Cheyenne got lucky

or George Custer's luck ran out. They hovered over
the grass, the rainbows, but my sons Matt & Scott

weren't looking in that direction. Not yet—I was
stopped to give them their American history lesson:

a little about General George Armstrong Custer, a lot
about having to fight on that June day. Matt told Scott

he wanted to know what it was to have died or worse
in those grasses. I'm sure Scott saw the rainbows first.

A rainbow is said to be the reminder of God promising
not to flood the world again. Two rainbows, twice that.

Categorically big. On the order of magnitude of healing
the entire unhappy planet & maybe the rest of Creation.

Not saying I left there changed, a different man. I am
saying I saw a double rainbow over a battlefield once.

Dead Flowers

was the song by the Rolling Stones on the player
the night Don Surratt reached over & cranked it up.
We'd pulled a double shift at Walker Manufacturing,

& it was time to smoke some hashish. We parked just
long enough to get good & wrecked in the high grasses
roadside with the windows of the car rolled up to seal

in a drummer who taught the rest of the band. But
he was right: the music was suddenly ever-present—
Jagger's ballsy vocals, Keith Richards' guitar vying

for a share of the listener's attention, & getting it.
The singer is asking not to be forgotten, only that—
I'm turning up the volume & thinking of you, Don.

It was your idea to pull over & to try & forget how
broken we are, the world always up to its ass in war
& or the famine of hope that precedes it. You said

to tell you about the Air Force, & so I did. However,
I had to turn the music down from maximum volume.
Now I think you'd join me in cranking up the music,

Russian tanks rolling into Ukraine. I hear you whisper-
shout to be heard over Time's unruly music: *This is
how you listen to "Dead Flowers" & the Stones!*

The Week the Whole World Got the Blues

That was the week Russia invaded Ukraine and rockets
landed in the towns where Ukrainian defenders gathered.
Story is, a Ukrainian captain told a Russian naval officer
challenged him in open seas, Fuck you. I was around
for the Cuban Missile Crisis in '62. So go on, Mr. Putin.
Put your nuclear arsenal on High Alert. Arrest pissed-off
thousands of Russians for violating the lie-narrative of the
military incursion, disagreeing with wide-reaching evil.

Doom is opening that Lego set with Rowan, my grandson
named for those who perished by the sword as often as not,
Vikings picturing Valhalla and slaughtering their neighbors.
What God asks us to lie that we are free, if freedom means
we are free to be wiped out in heart-shaped conflagrations
of nationalism? Fuck that. And fuck that God, too. Doom
is knowing that Rowan may see his life shortened by war,
my grandson with a great name and angel-face to match.

Did You Ever Feel Like You'd Seen *Bring Me the Head of Alfredo Garcia* One Time Too Many?

Sometimes a man is at the end of his rope and wants to escape.
Which is why he winds up in Mexico, though this piano player

is an American and has something to say about all the expatriate-
piano-player-down-on-his-luck drivel. Warren Oates plays Bennie—

we never get his last name because who cares; it's Mexico, after all.
In the course of things, he shoots a dead man over and over because

it feels good. Who am I to judge a bunch of children taking turns
stomping and setting fire to scorpions in another Peckinpah movie?

Who am I to overlook a world rife with creatures in need of killing?
Bennie is buried alive in one scene. In preparation, Oates downed

mushrooms. The hallucinogenic kind. He was two or three days
getting his head out of a shallow ersatz-grave, psychologically.

There's buried alive to dramatize lifelessness—call it acting—
and there's Warren Oates trying to out-Peckinpah, Peckinpah.

Flamenco

She described, over drinks, a style of sophisticated
dancing—I heard *Spain* and the word *flamenco* soft-
spoken in a voice gathers shut like a bud. Sometime

later, she recited a line from Federico Garcia Lorca:
A wall of difficult dreams / divides me from the dead.
I recall, now, how she let me hoist her onto my lap

in the Men's Room stall: we surprised a caretaker
struggling to unsee at least some of his life. I recall
it wasn't Spain, the flamenco, but we had a moment.

If there is a wall of dreams between the dead and us,
then I want to call up the sweet reek of her when lights
flickered and went out. That day, years before she died,

over our excited breathing, I heard dinosaur-harvesters
coughing out late-summer crop bundles. I want to hear
dream-walls between that woman and me collapse and

become engine-throttling-up noise and wheel-turning.
Maybe she'll want to dish the dirt about the afterlife.
Meaning how the dancing is after we stop breathing.

Living in Those Days before the World Ended

I knew we vessel hope, so I tried to be positive. To eat right
and exercise. I'd never seen a man's throat cut post mortem.
CNN footage said Russians did that to the Ukrainian dead.

After, I watched YouTube documentaries on nuclear war,
trying to learn if there was anything I could do; and, if so,
how to estimate survivability at a judicious distance from

the blast. But those who cut the throats of corpses before
rolling men, women, and children into mass graves need
their throats cut. Their denuded bodies left for the crows.

What did documentaries say? That we were fucked, given
our location. Most, if not all, of the survivors in a Southern
Hemisphere clouded by fallout events after the exchanges.

In one documentary, an elderly Japanese man testified he
survived both bombs dropped. Hiroshima and Nagasaki.
At Hiroshima, he leapt into a culvert. The detonation

washed over him. The man said he counts himself lucky.
If delusional thinking was religious experience, we'd all
be washed-in-the-blood pure and on our way to Heaven.

Apocalypse Note Found on a Whirlpool Refrigerator Door in Pataskala, Ohio

I'm sorry I ate everything.
Not a plum or a pomegranate

anywhere in this hell house—
plums were never safe around me.

Go outside. Find a wheelbarrow.
The one glazed with rain if it's

raining—did you come this far
to need a note from a dead man?

In the words of the guitar player
who lives up the road in Dublin,

the great Eric Clapton: *Plant
your love and let it grow.* Did

you think dream imagine that
the past would feed you forever?

The Reincarnation of Paul Revere's Horse

See the patriot with the tricornered hat,
a silversmith's hands. See the horse fall.

See the silversmith, like any rolling stone,
cartwheeling, suddenly unsaddled, horse-

carcass rising, wobblingly. Reanimating.
See the Son of Liberty run a hand through

the bloodied mane as if doubting himself,
miracle like new reins to the amazed rider;

all that freedom-prattle misplaced on these
on a mission to rouse the sleeping citizenry

and now, perchance, the arbitrary clemency
of a deity who has won a bet with the angels,

saying, in that heaven-come-to-earth voice,
With the bit in its mouth, and still saddled.

Protesters in Kayaks Chain Themselves
to Russian Oil Tanker

This was the same day the oldest person in the world,
a Japanese woman named Kane Tanaka, died at 119—
the kayaks of the Norwegians in stark contrast to a tanker
carrying 100,000 metric tons of light sweet crude for Esso.

Greenpeace of Norway had bannered OIL FUELS WAR
(in English) as Kane Tanaka eased from her REM sleep
to a more profound sleep before lifting from the body
like a Russian tanker on rough seas. Photographs

of a mammoth ship and a trio of chartreuse kayaks
include a rust-heavy anchor chain as if that great
weight is about equal to the love required to lift
so peacefully, and finally, up and up and, yes,

out of physicality and sentience—so gently
we overlook how the Engine works, how
a moment is fueled and what outcomes
may indeed follow in its bright wake.

Ghoul Steals 95-Year-Old Alistair Cooke's Bones before Cremation

> ...*The New York Daily News* quoted sources as saying that
> Mastromarino allegedly changed Cooke's cause of death to a
> heart attack and changed his age from 95 to 85 in paperwork
> given to two processing companies.
> —MSNBC.com

You could say he's the sort of Brooklynite we all fear—
one who can quote you street price for a cadaver femur.

There's a documentary of a shaved-head telling us how
he and an accomplice used PVC pipe to fill out each leg.

They harvested tissue from a good 1000 dead New Yorkers,
including Alistair Cooke, voice of PBS' Masterpiece Theatre—

how would you like to be told your 95-year-old dead loved one
was what you scattered but with a bit of PVC pipe in there, too?

Footage ends with the jump-suited inmate crying crocodile tears
and pleading good intentions since he has truly screwed the pooch.

Who but God decides how All of Creation behaves, so it's on Her—
or we're alone here and praying not to die anywhere in Brooklyn.

If ever anyone prayed for there to be no Hell, after, this is that dude:
someone who looks into a camera in a New York prison Visitors

Area to say that he loves America and his mother, a voice-over
saying she long ago disowned him, a heart being only so big.

Knights Inn

The guy before him hanged himself. Or that's what Columbus
police labeled the death. Suicide. He got hired saying he didn't

mind sleeping in the dead guy's bed. Ray-Ray likes to be called
Ray-Ray. Says friends call him that. He propagandizes the free

lollipops by coffee urns. The Plexiglass shield set someone back—
Ray-Ray's **John & Yoko: War Is Over** T-shirt is appropriately

ironic, given what's happening to Ukrainians. Twenty days now.
The woman with the kid has a magnificent afro. A leopard-motif

Spring dress that might be a second skin. As if on cue, her child
takes off running. The woman watches Ray-Ray run her card.

CNN is on the small screen behind the Plexiglass, and Ray-
Ray comments on war crimes Russia has committed, chief

among them bombing a maternity hospital and an orphanage.
Now a Russian reporter upstages with a placard of truth, writing

NOWAR (in English) as if it's one word and a state of mind.
The woman calls to the child who comes to her and stands,

fidgety and inattentive and tugging at the hem of her dress,
looking up as if into the Face of Love or God or maybe both.

Apology to Yeti, Who Made the Trip from Columbus, Ohio, to Bend, Oregon, in David Pryor's Chevy Van That Summer

I was 23 and full of myself. Young, angry white guy.
Married. No kids yet, and in my second year of college.
A week-away fledgling men (including me) would kill for,
though you managed to soak my sleeping bag in the heat

every straw-hat mile we drove, the doggie-waterfalls of
slobber pouring forth. Nothing trivial about you, pup.
It was blistering that summer, but we were both new
to the world, you and me. David and Jimmy, too.

If I had been able to drive a stick shift, I'd have
been sitting up front. But it was just you and me.
So forgive my shoving your Great Pyrenees heft.
What's one sleeping bag, you beautiful dog you.

And I want to apologize if I crowded you, dude.
David tells me you're gone—I will be soon, too.
Or it feels like that sometimes this far from 1977
and that sweet July we were young together, Yeti.

Heart Shaped World

That was one of the songs I listened to then: Chris Isaak.
His music would have been in my forebrain partying with
Stan Plumly around the time he called me Reverend Roy.

It was after a reading he gave. We were at David Baker's.
I'd published books of poems. Won a few awards. You
don't have to think it's a heart-shaped world, but it is.

Curtains and sheers pull-tied to either side, last light
splashed a Harley's black tank and fenders, and Stan
gestured outside. He queried, Yours? and I nodded.

I recalled the poem to a student of his, a suicide he
knew: *What or who she saw at the bottom of her fall
matters less than the weight of pain she carried there.*

Stan Plumly was from Barnesville: Wheeling but on
the Ohio side. And, if we are what we eat and drink,
he was three-fourths foul water: a body as the blood

in a heart-shaped world where we are what we are.
Used-up either side, but at all times the same river.
I see him stand off from the noisy rest of us, maybe

triaging certainties to risk on strangers. How much
approbation to share within earshot of eavesdroppers.
Leaving the drive that night, sure, I revved the engine.

God Hears Her Favorite Robert Plant
Alison Krauss Song "Can't Let Go"

If I'm God, then I must be All Life and, therefore, Lovely.
Maybe Tom Wait's Redhead in a Uniform or the Mona Lisa.
You kidding? I caught a look at myself walking by a storefront.

Your Maker is some shit. I thought of the poem by the guy
says to love your life since that particular DNA arrangement
is one of a kind, singular. Phil Levine: Old Man Levine's boy.

I'm sorry, but all of my jokes are dad-jokes to humans. And
oh, yeah—Robert Plant isn't Divinity. Alison Krauss, either.
But you have to be astonished at any two angels, don't you?

Bluegrass Meets "Stairway to Heaven"—as satisfying as sex.
I would appreciate a little gratitude for coming up with fucking.
So, nothing? Just that response is why I left so much Nothing.

Fine. But you bitches had better start praying to Yours Truly
that my favorite song these days remains "Can't Let Go"
or you really are screwed—can you say Armageddon?

Nineteen Seventy-four

Someone is putting
down the needle onto a spinning record, just so.
—Rick Barot, "Ode with Interruptions"

Someone is making pina coladas in the kitchen,
grinding ice drowning out someone cursing Nixon.
A small Black woman says this is her 21st birthday.
She opens a fifth of something she lights a shot of.

Someone in elephant bellbottoms and a great afro
is lighting a woman's cigarette. The woman pulls
down her minidress and smiles at the guy with the
match. There's someone who could be me at twenty.

That's him—the guy changing the records. Holding
shiny vinyl by the edges. Using some antistatic once
the platter is on the turntable. A record is there now,
though its carrier was unsteady his last steps through

a hazy room. He has inhaled his share and then some.
What could the guy want to hear so badly at midnight
in the absence of night breezes? Etta James, I guess,
since Etta James is starting "At Last" as if America

might still be that cool breeze we wait for. At last—
see the Tina Turner poster over the diamonded door?
Stand here a moment and watch the headlamps pass,
the lines of trailers light up. Watch as Tina Turner's

parted-thighs remind us that's where we come from:
stardust, or so says Joni Mitchell in that song of hers:
four-billion-year-old carbon that distinguished itself
at least well enough to hang around here for a while.

Honesty

My wife Gloria and I have been married
for 25 years. Yesterday, I confessed to her,
saying something I said someone else said

had been invented: I told her a high schooler
next door called me Old Man. I said I'd lied
and that the lie was wholly for her benefit—

I told her that Dominick (whose name means
"belonging to the Lord") tossed me a regulation-
sized NFL leather football in a damn-tight spiral.

Without mentioning that I was anything but
someone in a yard catching a football in May.
The lie was me doing my best to tell her I was

certain (or as certain as you get after a while)
that there was a realistic likelihood she'd laugh,
and hard, at anyone calling me Old or Old Man.

She did laugh. One of those authentic-to-a-fault
guffaws you remember like your spouse's birthday.
Certainly, now I have That Unrepeatable Moment

and the truth about how hard it is to love and feel
you belong anywhere—which I intend to hand her
as replacement for an honest-to-God perfect card.

Death Row Soundtrack

Life can be bright in America
If you can fight in America
Life is all right in America
If you're all white in America
                    —"America," *West Side Story*

The next executioner you see in this poem will be wearing coveralls
with Executioner in the name-egg on the pocket. She will be humming

the ditty from *West Side Story*: the idea that there's no shame in being
a witness to an execution. Or the executioner. The executioner is eager

to share a smile after a shock of recognition at the phrase *Everything's
free in America,* irony in evident attendance. Big ol' death-house grin.

She says she keeps score: So many smiles, so many fuck-yous. And
that she'll tell you how many of each, if you promise not to judge—

I mean, what self-respecting executioner is going to be humming the
showtune with a lyric that life is all right in America if you're white?

They're dour—One Tough Room, honestly—and oppressed but are
bearing up under the weight of the day. She says it's worth it to see

a smile in the Death House. Beauty has its place. And humor. And
neither beauty nor humor is free. There's nothing free in America.

The Ghost of the Hunchback of Notre Dame Assesses Mick Jagger

These days, I'm approximately deaf from the truth of the bells.
Even if I crank up the volume knob on the TV, I can only feel

the great Keith Richards building the Church of Sound and Fury.
Oh, and don't act like hearing is just the one thing. Any bellringer

worth his wage will tell you that what we lose is compensated for.
On one wall of this bar, there he is: Sir Mick, quintessentially him,

answering what to do with this body and a stalwart, beating heart.
Esmeralda purrs, *He's some shit, don't you think?* Don't ask me

questions you don't want to hear the answer to. I tell her I see
Charles Laughton minus a few pounds: Laughton played me

in a movie of the Victor Hugo novel. Esmeralda says
it grows on you, rock 'n roll. Like faith. But then,

she was hanged after my protection failed, a veteran
of discovering no one gets much satisfaction anymore.

Starman

Crash-landed between stands of hardwoods, he exits
a space capsule in Levis and high-top basketball shoes

and a t-shirt repeating John Lennon: *God Is A Concept*
By Which We Measure Our Pain. There's a lake. But

he knows walking on water may draw one-sided stares,
so he swims, shaking off reentry's customary battering.

A circular contusion on his bare alien arm is healing
in the shape of the Seal of the Great State of Ohio—

cabin lights are a summoning akin to the last-wish
Any Dry Ground of drowning sailors. The sooner

he does what he's sworn to do, the sooner he returns
to wife and kids. Swimming, he visualizes her. Them.

He stands, sodden with Wonder and feeling that, here,
all joy starts with stepping over a sea of plastic bottles.

Hymns without the Messiah-Christ-Jesus
or that Show-Patter about the Resurrection

Hymns like those aren't about reclamation as much as
about thinking for oneself. You know, not buying Grace,
the Virgin Birth, or the worship of an assortment of saints.
No self-respecting deity representative of the idea of Good
could be associated with concepts like eternal punishment.
More than a tad over-the-top, especially for a merciful God.

Priests of the Old Gods drove a hard bargain when it comes
to the mollification of sin by means of blood sacrifice: I read
the Romans sacrificed bulls and rams to Jupiter, letting blood
be poured over them, literally, in any of the countless temples.
Wouldn't it have been better to take a stab at sublimity without
having to be bathed in the blood of even one innocent creature?

Flannery O'Connor visualized the Catholic Jesus of Nazareth,
while admitting to having the hots for rocketeer Gus Grissom.
I remember her Hazel Motes trying on faith and redemption
like a new coat. Theology that included forgiveness canceling
Original Sin in favor of all the souls that have been (or ever
will be) sidestepping hellfire. No? Then show me zip codes

or the GPS coordinates for a lost paradise Milton imagined,
the inferno-purgatorio-paradiso in Dante's *Divine Comedy*.
We're born into a black-hole-littered Universe. Lighten up.
I offer as alternative: Open your hymnbooks to page 369—
Patti Smith: "Because the Night"—*because the night
belongs to lovers because the night belongs to us.*

And There Fell a Great Star from Heaven

I was taught to read from the last book in the Bible,
so I'm told or so my grandmother used to remind me.
My grandmother Potter. As in, Frances Collier Potter.
Phrases like *And there fell a great star from Heaven*

were mine to decipher for this woman who praised
my third-grade mispronunciations, saying, yet again,
how third grade was as far as she'd gotten in school.
Whatever was in the plague-vials archangels poured

on the earth, it registered. The gorgeous story of it.
Asleep, I'd see winged shapes. She had me hooked.
This was years before I could tell a DC comic from
a Marvel. She had two sons shot dead in Kentucky

bar fights—I can't forget that. Meaning I might hear
I place you in God's hands. She wanted to see me
protected. Maybe wrapped in marvel for a while
before Calamity claims us and we're gone.

She Begins to Dread the Finality of Arrival

—Julian Lucas, "Motherless Tongue" (*The New Yorker*)

My name's none of your business. I'm a prisoner for
the reason I did my best to shoot someone who needed
shot. Fortunately, it wasn't my gun. I missed. Six times.

Furloughs are few and far between at Eastern, especially
if you're a woman with a doctor-brother who some judge
a court in Whitesburg says has the say-so. Women aren't

to express exasperation, compliance the goal of therapies.
I managed a furlough at Christmas, Brother picking me up
in a hearse customized in case he needed to use restraints—

which he had to do when the time arrived to come back here
after my last leave. I did all right exiting the asylum grounds,
but return was impossible to agree to. A cloud of red-temper

came over me like a curtain drawn closed. I don't remember
hitting Brother. But he told them I did, and in front of others.
Says I called him terrible names. Which sounds about right.

Especially since he sold off our parents' best bottomland
without my consent. I'd claw his eyes out of his head, if
it didn't mean I'd never get out of this hellish institution,

where they call tortures Treatment and administer them
without authorization. Not to mention the other residents
who giggle at your humiliation, happy it's not their turn.

If I want anything but furloughs, I have to watch myself.
There are things far worse than being put in handcuffs
and having both legs cinched down so you can't kick.

White American Light

My window is, first, a matter of seniority.
I came to be here as a much younger woman.
A window was worth coming to blows over.

Enough of the history of the country. Look there.
That stripe of leafing trees, in some lightscapes,
is like living after profound disappointment—

like good luck had franchised near you, but
you hadn't yet gotten the hang of accessing it.
The floorwalker tells me those are honey locusts.

Whatever they are, they block out a countryside
of too-shiny, finned cars. Cadillacs with families
of hillbillies flush with a year of factory wages—

but then, this is just one story that's happening
in what James the floorwalker here on 4 West
has christened *White American Light*, saying

I'm the Wicked Girl who needs to be punished.
In due course, we all pay up. But that isn't love
in the dead eyes of the floorwalker who knows

how everything American appears to have begun
with a paradise-in-progress hard landing of ships
and a brief argument about where to bury bodies.

Poem in Praise of Surviving My Life

—after Vijay Seshadri

A tire struck the windshield and I was killed,
at once decapitated, both my dead eyes staring
at the sun-saccharine oblivion of summer-green
West Virginia. Or—as an alternative, here I am,
living on as if nothing had happened. Oh, there

is still an awful accident, but I survive it—
still the father of the woman beside me, Cait,
who will yet gift me a grandson—the Last
Viking Prince, I might have called him,
if I'd unbelievably avoided the blow

of the errant truck tire bouncing toward me
and so am both here and alive. Part of the less
expected future beyond—or quite simply lifeless:
blood and more blood at such and such a mile marker,
the Florida-shirted driver up from Florida, destination-

Ohio the next metaverse of hill and interstate highway.
It's astonishing. Pieces of Yours Truly scattered over
the interior of the convertible my wife had to have:
breath leave-taking a ruined body as if all life
is, first, what might have been then was.

Doozy Machina

My wife doesn't hate gangster films, though she's Sicilian.
Meaning she takes a measure of pride in being what she is
but never feels quite accepted in her own country. Anyway,
we're watching an appallingly bad gangster film. Which is
set after a nuclear war or a sort of plague. We're watching
with the subtitles turned on, so that we can both hear and
double-check the dialogue. She catches *deus ex machina*—
"god out of the machine" mistranslated as *doozy machina*.
I know where *doozy* comes from because my father and I

once built a model of the Duesenberg Model SJ from a kit:
*They used to say something was a Duesy. Meaning it was
amazing or one of a kind—hand me that tube of Testor's.*
My father's favorite chrome-silver Zippo had a flame that
deflated with a sudden click if he was pissed. I remember
dry-fitting parts: the 1932 Duesy limo with its Lycoming
Straight-8 motor and white sidewall tires—running boards
made movie-famous by Prohibition bootleggers and crooks.
I recall he got pissed at the process or some mistake I made

and aimed a burning cigarette at the floor. It bounced, his
lit L&M, up from the floor of his electronics repair shop.
Star sparks of burning Virginia tobacco and paper flying,
I thought the world had ended or was about to. I cried.
Testor's glue makes you loopy in enclosed rooms, so
maybe he was loopy from breathing glue-fumes. Still,
he was tough and he had a doozy / Duesy of a temper—
like my Sicilian-American wife Gloria, he was someone
I'm sure felt somewhat displaced in adopted-home Ohio.

If there was a god in the machines he fixed, I never saw it.
And he used to say Dayton, Ohio was a doozy, my father.
He liked it well enough. Or he was being sarcastic, as in:
It's one doozy of a wrecked world, but it'll do, won't it?
Now, I ask my wife for the remote. Kill the captioning.

She tells me not to dialog through the narrative. Not to assume she hears what I hear. Not to assume anything. After, we give a post-apocalyptic, racketeer-shitscape America our allegiance and our undivided attention.

Laughing Out Loud at the End of the World

The End of the World is happening in a Kroger Superstore,
where unmasked shoppers in Crocs make supermarket runs.

Just look at the cabbie with a landslide of hamburger meat.
If he's an Uber for the elderly and therefore sanctified, he's

nonetheless barking up the wrong tree, concluding the high
probability of an After after a nuclear exchange—if not fire-

and blast-damage, then ruined air leaking radiation and death.
My hillbilly-refugee pops worked for the government, a GS-11

who calibrated guidance systems for ICBMs. He said his work
was to ensure warheads could be aimed accurately. He bragged

they could deliver a payload through a specific building window
after a 6000-mile journey to parts of Russia. He seemed pleased

at the capability of what he was part of, accurately adjusting
this or that thingamajig to faithfully announce Fuck You—

like the guy who, without hesitation, grabs what he needs
as if the End of the World is another day in the Midwest.

Harry Potter & the Several Pissed-off Velociraptors

No animagi are poised to rescue Harry.
Velociraptors don't answer to incantations

post-dating the Jurassic. And neither shaggy-
bearded Hagrid nor Dumbledore are defense

against predation of this order of magnitude—
which is to say, what's a little offering of flesh

between friends? What's a smallish foretaste
before the entree and bread-sticks? Look—

check what's eyeballing Our Hero as if he's
some fundraiser Hors d'oeuvre or finger food.

See it purse its reptilian lips and lip-sync Dude.
Maybe someone should clarify the rules. Some

redundant walk-on confident in Velociraptor
or whatever dead language the dead whisper.

Ron has pissed his Tommy Johns, Hermione
a Victoria Secret body stocking. Nonetheless,

main characters (like Harry) are off the menu,
Story superseding any clear and present danger.

Still, see Harry's hand wobble as if the wand he
commands had turned considerable all at once.

And in the Naked Light I Saw

—Paul Simon, "The Sound of Silence"

First of all, a country on its phones:
AI-juried Facebook commentary on
the screen-time autobiographies of my

stupid-joy and that of many others. Next,
I saw swarms of us moving for no reason.
I saw a country needing shown the truth

about wealth and treasure and its treasure
hunters: that every fortune is underwritten
by organized graft or quasi-legal robbery.

Show me a fortune, I'll show you a thief.
To quote everyone and Pink Floyd: *Keep
your hands off of my stack.* Or to quote

the Great Tom Waits: *See, a redhead
in a uniform will always get you horny.*

Bouquets at Your First Funeral Were Nothing Compared to the Histrionics at Your Last

Of course arrangements of red roses
proliferated, chrysanthemums and lilies.
And sentiment on the first round of cards
was unanimous in praising your lived life.

The words rang with an easy sentimentality.
You can almost hear hymns wherein Heaven
and Mary midwife White Power nationalism.
They left the dead fetus inside you. Plumped

your bosom at that showing. The mortician,
in all cases, received praise. It is hard when
your job is hard but doesn't appear to be so.
They say that your breathing grew labored

as during great exertion or sexual climax—
the latter memorial was the most weighty
for the wailing, the lovers feeling the loss
like a sloughing off of burned second-skin.

We Were Drinking Kentucky Bourbon

The Supreme Court had annulled *Roe v. Wade.*
Drinking was called for, but not in celebration—
I was thinking of Ava Gardner who simply flew

to London, three times, to abort Sinatra's child.
I was remembering a student at a college in Ohio,
who presented me some pro-life iPhone photograph,

saying, Why isn't taking its life an act of homicide?
I told her if it was killing, we'd need a punishment.
I stood rattling off a definition of murder, kidding

how it can't be homicide if Ava Gardner does it.
Mick Jagger made it crystal clear: *I shouted out*
Who killed the Kennedys? / when, after all, it

was you and me. Today, I toast what I want to.
This is my toast asking, So you want to decide
what Ava Gardner does with her body? There

are Bible verses on womanly subjugation which
the American Christians can quote. Nevertheless,
when have most men been otherwise? When have

they ever regarded women as being free humans?
You don't have to drink much to feel something.
You don't have to be a Rolling Stone to be free.

Dinosaurs May Have Been Killed Off by a Comet

They call men who see women as playthings dropped here
on Planet Earth in the Milky Way Galaxy for the delight
of men, dinosaurs. Such men raised me, but I've done

what I could to make sure that death isn't preferable
to a life of lockdowns with Yours Truly. Nonetheless,
now the subject is the late-Jurassic. The reporter says it

comes down to microclimate. Risk is what it is to live.
We see forests of ferns and hear an overvoice speaking.
Though it is difficult to put this in words in the middle

of a poem about all that reptilian death—I ask, love,
for you to take my longing, in the absence of anything
like security. In this burning house of trying to live—

there's really nothing to be done, is there? By dinosaur
or man, by flowering plant or cotyledon-esurient nemesis.
If a similar act-of-chance, gravitational fuckery occurred

tomorrow—a big mega-dollop of Ocean kersplashed as high
as the Empire State Building, the planet zapped to extinction—
what difference could it make, walking in a neighborhood,

to know it was likely the last time you'd walk anywhere?
Better to be caught midstep. Swept along. Gently at first.

"Take It Easy"

I never cared for Bernie Leadon or his banjo,
having seen The Eagles live in Memphis once
as opening act for Yes—who were burning up
the Top-40 charts. "Take It Easy" was on AM,

in what we used to refer to as Repeated Rotation.
Woody Cross bought the tickets. And he drove us.
He said he knew where we could get some Smoke,
but it was in Mississippi. He felt about Mississippi

like I felt about the banjo—nothing shouts White
Power like the whatsit patterned on West African
plucked spike lutes and popularized by blackface
minstrelsy. I saw Black abductees shuffle-march,

shoeless, in chains, onto a pine-plank welcoming.
Saw an overseer expose a wineskin, downing big
monster-swallows, whip in hand, to banjo music—
Woody's folks said, Stay out of Mississippi. Said

it comes down to the world being a wrecked place.
They clarified it had to do with unrest that summer.
Which did seem to be on Repeated Rotation. They
said it wasn't safe. Woody's godawful-purple '72

Gremlin was all windshield. A grin filled my side
as we drove past burned-out downtown Memphis.
Both of us staggeringly high because, of course,
we'd, by no means, stayed out of Mississippi.

The Hill Rises, Cresting

> She is not thinking about this at all. She is thinking
> about the coins knotted in the bundle beneath her hands.
> —*Light in August*, William Faulkner

It was my idea to get an ice cream from the truck.
I hollered at that rascally Bobby, disappearing, and

daughter Nettie's boy Roy right behind him. But I had
thought to snatch up two embroidered handkerchiefs—

one of knotted quarters, Walking Liberty half dollars.
I ran after the boys, who were out and gone and so

mine to catch. Which is what I was doing when I felt
an ache in my chest. Over the heart. Got lightheaded.

Still, I stepped on it and caught them—did I mention
Nettie and husband Roy, Senior had a house on a hill?

All the *I Love You, Granny* in the world can't make up
for a hill and having to mind grandkids—did I mention

I coughed blood? I'm sure I filled the other handkerchief.
I blamed Bobby, but both boys caused it. May I just say,

across Time Without End and what attends the Soul after,
they were lucky I had enough change for three ice creams.

Trigger (Left) and Roy Rogers (Right)

That's what the caption of the fan-photograph reads,
as if you couldn't tell the difference between a horse

and its hominid rider. If we're asleep, America,
dreaming a dream of Independence at Any Price,

why should slaughter in the thoroughfare wake us?
Wasn't it indiscriminate carnage bought the place?

When Trigger died in 1965, Roy had his Golden
Palomino stallion's skin professionally stretched

across a gutta-percha-and-wire likeness. Which
is fucked up: crazy on the order of magnitude of

Crazy comparable to changing your name to Roy
and buying the mendacities of our history. Horses

like Trigger deserve better. Still, it takes one of us
to make the Fantastic real—which is why, as a kid,

you dropped off to sleep at Christmas on Comanche
Drive in your cowboy get-up. Content, if not blissful.

Dead Johnny Cash Tells Us Where-all He's Been

Dead Johnny has been everywhere by virtue of the fact
the dead get to move the fuck around, don't you know.
They float over Tucson or Tucumcari, Tehachapi or
Tonopah with approximately equal ease, regardless.

In his case, Cash left behind concert recordings and
a reputation for being a good moral man, and a patriot.
And so, DJC has this gig earns him an audience among
the living; it's his voice in an ad for the USPS, which

Dead Johnny is saying needs our applause and support.
And for that, he gets his ass the equivalent of resurrected
and earns—who says America is just a grift for the rich?
who says the dead can't get in on a little of that action?

Truth is, the living Johnny Cash worked as a postman.
DJC rattles off a bunch of North American city names.
I'll spare you the sassy-song-lyric-alliteration-in-lieu-
of-geographical-information, but he's been *everywhere*.

More the Smoky Voice of Longing and Loss

—Billy Collins, "The Invention of the Saxophone"
from *The Art of Drowning*

On one wall of my father's Shell-station office is
the Genuine Auto Parts calendar for 1962 and a price
chart for major repairs and routine vehicle maintenance.
The price chart has a grease-pen on a string for changes;
the pen sways with gusts in the winter or if it's storming.
The fire-engine-red, halved-bell ringer is pegged to a wall
by the cash register. There are three or four plastic chairs
for customers, depending on how rowdy the mechanics

and pump-jockeys have gotten between jobs: the usual
consequences of their locker room grab-ass passed on
to Pops who chalks it up to the cost of doing business.
He tells me to watch—if they wrestle and roughhouse.
Says chairs are replaceable. And not to tell my mother,
a cautionary ask he delivers in a low voice and smiling.
I've no trouble seeing myself shanghaied at the house
where the news is of JFK. Russian missiles in Cuba.

Pops has a postman-friend (Buster) who will stop by
after he finishes his route. And if it's autumn, Buster
is sucking down a 7Up and bullshitting about women.
My father's name, spelled out on the station window,
says what it says in red-white-and-blue script lettering.
Soon it will be closing time at Roy's Shell. Buster will
want to lead the way up Woodman Drive to a Parkmoor
where both know the veteran waitresses. If it's pay day,

Buster and Pops race the whole way. He has cop friends,
my father, should he get stopped. He's white. A veteran
of a war fought before he and Mother married and I was
born in a Dayton hospital named for the Good Samaritan.
Nevertheless, the top is down on the XKE. October-Ohio

wears scents of manure and Old Spice. I'm 8 and wonder
if the Cosmos is able to distinguish shit from man-smell,
my father from the other dead if the sky should explode.

Brubaker Extra Lobbies the Third-shift Janitors

A dollop of sun above the air force station fence line,
a lot of the third-shift janitors are about to clock out.
Some stand. Some are sitting on a concrete barricade.
Quite a few are smoking. One in a Stones t-shirt says
people he drinks with at a bar are scouting for extras.
This bastard mocks me whenever he remembers to—
he's awash in a wallow of first light, bragging how
he met movie-star Robert Redford. Shook his hand.

He horselaughs like America is, on the whole, fair.
A stone's throw from a big Stars & Stripes, the guy
is animated when he talks acting, but he manages
to get fired that summer for stealing toilet paper.
If the world is a stage, a life our hour upon it—
this is his, the thief whose name I've forgotten.
Someone looking for this shit-life to mean more,
having forgotten he was a janitor, and in Ohio.

What Being the Target of a Dragon's Heat and Flame Teaches Us

That you don't have to live like a refugee until you do.
That myth is myth and oodles of lying until it isn't.

That some take seriously Compassionate Endings,
setting the curve for the scoring of other divinities

(in both classroom and laboratory) since exiting here
by sudden-and-surprising immolation is drive-through

cremation and an end-of-life option in some multiverses.
That Freedom of Speech has limits and consequences and

that even the Good Guys must be prepared to step lively—
that you can bargain for mercy with some beasts, that some

kill and grin like certain breeds of dog where the mouth says
that there are states of mind approaching wonderment where

words like *tragedy* get tossed around as the odors downwind
supplant seasonal smells of chance wild plants and rain scent.

It's all fun in the name of Make-believe until someone gets
singed, burned, the char blathering about fairness and pity.

Hillbilly

The word *hillbilly* would as soon fight as fuck.
My sister Suzanne is telling me she won't allow
the word vocalized in her Ohio home. Her call.
It's a quote racial slur unquote against white folk-
hillbillies, and our parents were as Appalachian
as it gets—meaning that she's injured by the word.
Suzanne would tell you, I don't say it myself. Her
brother, however, is honored to be an Appalachian,
my DNA convened by the chemistries of residence.

For me, it's not about pissing off psycho-America.
The designation *hillbilly* identifies us as the cosmic
goofs we are. Accidents of neither grace nor design.
The world is so much bigger than language, isn't it?
My sister was born under a bad sign or something.
Nevertheless, the word *hillbilly* would respond by
reminding us that to express anything restricts its
meaning. Which arises out of the nature of words,
those snarling motherfuckers spoiling for a fight.

Hillbilly Purgatory

No way they were going straight to Paradise
or Hell, whatever abyss they imagined earning.
So what if being really lost doesn't mean much.
Signs are misspelled and so more recognizable.
They enfranchise compunctious Americanisms,
their principal beauty the mercy of misdirection.
By the road's edge, Burma Shave signs swell the
air as if *all right* is categorically, and forever, two
English words. As the poet Theodore Roethke says,

A man goes far to find out who he is. And of course
no one with testes and a nutsack ever asks directions,
a majority of the dead slouching toward some iteration
of Bethlehem to be reborn as rock-climbing quadrupeds
free from sparkling cities of men and martyrs for a while.
This is their neighborhood no matter how it has changed.
An old woman accepts an L & M, the courtesy of a light.
And then, against her better judgment, asks what day it is
and if it's all right that she doesn't give a good goddamn.

Blood to the Bridles of the Horses

Which is how granny Potter poetically described
the combat on the plains of Armageddon, the setting
in the last book in the New Testament where one third
of the combatants in the world's militaries are slaughtered.
She'd quote from verses where they're talking winepresses.
She struggled to pass it off as canonical, accepted, her brash

embellishment that blood spilled would reach to the bridles
of make-believe horse regiments. At 5, I didn't doubt her.
But nowhere in The Book of Revelation does it say that.
There is mention of a third of the militaries being wiped
out but that's in the Book of Daniel, and has zilch-zero
to do with the gore that would entail. Nothing like that.

No such macabre additions, Mazy Frances Collier Potter.
Which means my third-grade-educated granny from the
hollows of east-Kentucky jazzed it up for her grandson,
skirting how disturbing allegories spawn bad dreams.
More likely, she had no idea of the power of her words.
For sure, she was conflating one prophet's delusional

thinking with another. She was such a true believer.
Being hillborn, a survivor of the coal wars, she knew
the rulebooks of the road say what we agree they say.
Better that a child's screams go out across all the years
of the rest of his life and the lives of his children than he
be caught off guard. That must have been her rationale.

Grieving

It assumes an audience of listeners in the hereafter.
It continues with a séance and a Ouija board where

the planchette is a heart-shaped, plastic valentine—
that thingamajig on the tabletop is as old as a fear

of death. There is a pencil remnant to help with
our suspicion of the occult and automatic writing;

that is to say, if the Spirits choose to make it slide,
it will write, and in American English, in this case,

creating a communiqué from beyond the Last Veil.
Something born of silence and abiding absence.

I could say it gets better, missing the dead. It doesn't.
You're heartsick, you carry doom like a rabbit's foot.

Rangoon Red

Ford Motor Company called its brightest red
Rangoon Red—maybe Ford Motor Company knew
what to expect to happen in Southeast Asia in nineteen
sixty-four, the year Nettie Bentley bought a new car.
But that was the color of the two-door Ford sedan,
one with *galaxy* misspelled in a chromed fender.
The car was new. Which is to say, never used.

Like the damned baby shoes in Hemingway's
six-word short story of unthinkable loss:
For sale: Baby shoes, never worn.
This was when lipstick was mostly
some variation of blood-colored and
she'd divorced my father for infidelity.
My mother was working second shift at

Inland Manufacturing, on Third in Dayton,
cutting GM trim strips for good UAW wages.
I recall the rose-colored cheek bruise she gave
my father, once, over another woman. He was
delivering me to the house she had in Kettering.
He said something about the car; made her mad,
and she dragged the other woman from his car.

I saw my mother strike her like the recognition
love can end and then recommence. It turns out,
no one likes being fucked with after buying a car.
It turns out, history is what it is and some sad shit.
Lots of getting cherry-red in the face and knocking
the hell out of someone you love. Oh, and strangers.
Anyone female and gutsy enough to sit beside him.

Bodies in Moonlight in Illinois

Light falling on the Midwest is adulterated,
according to the America West pilot who
said, once upon a time, there are three
levels of cloud cover above Chicago—

still, I remember opening a door
in a trailer in Rantoul, Illinois, and
seeing the momentary nature of light
assume the shape of lovers the coffee-

bronze of ancient pennies. My roommate
and a young woman from Philly, her red afro
another kind of starlight and oblivion altogether.
And I remember closing their door after passing

a message from the USAF hospital at Chanute:
someone in the chain of command had decided
to test our readiness. I felt bad interrupting them.
Most days, flesh is just flesh. This wasn't that.

I envied those fortunate lovers their portion
of a flood of March moonlight. I envied my
roommate his allocation of joy. Not saying
I begrudged him being Black in America.

Meanwhile, in the Afterlife

Researchers investigate possible transitional phase
between life and death…
                                        —Internet headline, 12/27/2024

Could be you're bouncing a grandson or -daughter
on one knee and Imminent Catastrophe on the other.
Meanwhile, in the afterlife your maternal grandmother

leans over a celestial balcony-railing to assay the results
of her hard work raising you. Mazy Frances Collier Potter—
she's buried children while a child herself. I'd tell you

if she waved to me, if I saw anything like that. However,
she hasn't. And her confidence about God and an afterlife
isn't mine. But I'm reimagining Granny in case she was

correctamundo about there being God. I reassemble her,
after years in the Kentucky earth. I'd ask her to treat life
like the possibility to catch a smoke. Drink from a flask.

If there is any justice in the Universe, if there ever was
or will be justice, she'll treat me like a child who hung
on her every word until her voice gave out and she

closed, with amazingly veined hands, the paperback
or Bible or comic book we were reading before sleep.
Eventually, she'll start to snore. Inside those noises,

I'll be safe or feel what's meant by words like *safe*.
And she'll be yet-alive, if there is a word for that.

Persons Not Riding Please Be
Off the Carousel Before it Starts

—background sign on an episode of *The Twilight Zone*

If anything on this planet is in short supply,
it's common sense—like the kind Uncle Billy
calls upon in *It's a Wonderful Life*, retracing his
steps, thinking Deliverance to be so near at hand
that all he has to do, next, is to reach out. Take it.
It's the day after Trump's second election victory,
and deliverance or no deliverance, common sense
or no common sense, a carousel of events seems
to want to reclaim a great deal more than our joy.
Whether it's Bedford Falls or *The Twilight Zone*,
what happens hereafter in America and the rest
of the world happens after we have overlooked

signs about our own daft-crazy uncle, if you will.
We're saying: Uncle Billy is a fool, but he's ours.
We may cheer for the big galoot as if for ourselves.
As if misplacing and so (by implication) pocketing
envelopes of money is plainly the nature of things.
Once a small kid got a leg mangled on a carousel.
Father was a judge. Member of the Masonic lodge.
After, this giant, red-lettered sign went up. Ignored
on the midway where the One True God resides and
the ride is always commencing. I guess I was saying
something that you didn't want to hear. Something
like: What in the living hell has gotten into you?

The One Life We've Been Given

I don't like imagining my life (or Being) adding up
to a Nothing Burger. Yeah, with cheese of exotic origin
but still nothing. My life would make a pretty good movie.
Movies are what we have in the United States of America
to save us from some poverty of Spirit. They're designed,

the movies, to deliver us for the cost of a ticket and popcorn.
Sort of like that one where everyone dies, *The Hateful Eight*.
If drive-in Westerns are anything, they're threatening. A man
almost gets gelded—that may be another movie where the life
we've been given is a gift until it isn't. If I had to point to my

flaws, I couldn't. Self-awareness seems to run from hillbillies
of North American descent. But if we met in a diner off I-70,
you alone in a booth beside a clock with Trump's wounding
on its face, me in a dead father's last full-length winter coat,
I hope you'd laugh at hearing that a film in which everyone

dies has that, at least, going for it. Might you be lonely and
hand me your number on a napkin of black-inked integers?
When I called, might I offer a Disney fairytale where Death
is reducible to the illumination in the eyes Old Yellering it
Elsewhere? Which is to say, anywhere along these roads.

Gimme Shelter

I'm confident that, when Mick and Keith Richards
were squeezing out this great song, they weren't
predicting Donald Trump fucking up America—
I have a friend who has to be overdosed on THC
to sit still for this shambolic *coup d' état*, though
he says things are the same as after the shootings
at KSU, when the Ohio National Guard opened fire
and other young Americans learned what Americans
keep learning: we're a vicious lot and not to be trusted.

It's in Merry Clayton's vocals releasing moral tension,
extending as a kind of petitioning. Call it an estimation
of how fucked we are—the singer's weeping moan—
but you don't need shelter until you've lost a home.
You don't have to be Keith Richards or Mick Jagger
to know about hard roads and about evil. This year
in Ohio, first rain sounds heartbreakingly tender
in the way grade-school crushes are tender—softly
malleable and as indefinite as honesty in some hands.

In the tradition of Billy Collins lying in grand fashion,
offering he had fished the Susquehanna when he hadn't,
that he didn't intend to fish it—saying he adored the way
the phrase sounded when read back—this isn't the year's
first rain. It's rained and snowed and hailed in the month
of December. January produced two measurable snowfalls,
but then Trump got sworn in and layoffs at NOAA began—
the National Oceanic and Atmospheric Administration has
posted alerts after, but fewer and fewer. We're making do

with the lack of truthfulness from our government, as we
did after the first reports of NVA dead and the Vietnamese
civilian casualties sometime in the Johnson Administration.
The country was built on slaughter, but don't press your luck.
If they opened the Hall of Fame of Transparent Lies and Liars,

Donald Trump would be ubiquitous in his attendance at the hall, if not a chief decider of the seating of guests and the mentors in the field of disingenuousness. Still, rain sounds like you expect rain should in winter in Ohio. Like the truth is we're in for it.

About the Author

Roy Bentley has published 11 books of poetry. He is the author of *Walking with Eve in the Loved City*, chosen by Billy Collins as finalist for the Miller Williams poetry prize; *Starlight Taxi*, winner of the Blue Lynx Poetry Prize; *The Trouble with a Short Horse in Montana*, chosen by John Gallaher as winner of the White Pine Poetry Prize. He's received fellowships from the National Endowment for the Arts, the Ohio Arts Council (6 times), and the Florida Division of Cultural Affairs. Poems have appeared in *New Letters, Prairie Schooner, december, Rattle, The Southern Review, Crazyhorse,* and *Shenandoah.*

Sheila-Na-Gig Editions